The Storytelling Architecture

Discover how to create exciting stories

with clever twists

A brief introduction:

Ever wonder how great stories are created?

How do writers and filmmakers manage to capture the audience's imagination and keep them engaged from start to finish?

If you are an aspiring writer, a filmmaker or simply someone who loves good stories, "The Architecture of Storytelling" is a must-read.

Written by a copywriter who has researched top storytelling experts.

This book offers deep insight into story creation.

Through a clear and concise approach, you'll learn narrative structure and how to use it to create compelling characters, exciting plots, and satisfying endings.

With practical examples and writing exercises, you'll be able to apply what you've learned to your own stories.

"The Architecture of Storytelling" is essential reading for anyone wanting to hone their writing skills and tell amazing stories.

Imagine an impressive building, with meticulous and detailed architecture…
Every column, every pillar, every arch has been carefully planned to ensure the structure is solid and imposing.

Now, imagine that building is not just a physical construction, but a story.

Just as architecture is the art and science of designing and building buildings, storytelling is the art and science of designing and building stories.

Every element of the story is carefully planned and structured to create an immersive and engaging narrative experience for the audience.

The foundation of the story is its structure. Just as the foundation of a building is the foundation that supports the entire weight of the structure, the structure of a story is what supports the entire plot.

The structure is composed of elements such as the beginning, middle and end, the central conflict, the twists and the climax.

As well as architectural elements such as columns and pillars, the structure of the story is reinforced by well-developed characters and dialogue.

Strong characters are like the mortar that holds the building's walls together, while well-written dialogue is like the decorative details that make the difference between a simple construction and a masterpiece.

And just as architecture can evoke emotions in visitors to a building, history can evoke emotions in its readers or spectators.

Careful choice of words, the atmosphere created and the way characters react to situations can influence the mood and emotions of the audience.

Just as well-designed architecture is a testament to the skill and vision of the architect, a well-told story is a testament to the skill and vision of the writer.

Storytelling is the architecture of the imagination, where each story is a unique and immortal construction that can transcend time and space and leave a lasting mark on the minds of those who experience it.

Summary:

- *Learn to structure your stories like a pro*
- *Create captivating characters that hold the audience's attention*
- *Develop gripping storylines that take audiences on an unforgettable journey*
- *Master the art of the twist and keep your audience engaged until the end*
- *Learn to create settings and environments that make your story come alive*
- *Develop a captivating and engaging writing style*
- *Discover how to use symbols and themes to add depth to your story*
- *The power of combination: How the three parts of the brain work together to wrap us up in a good story.*
- *Practical tips for revising and editing your story to make it perfect*

- *Create a satisfying ending that leaves the audience satisfied and thrilled*

Learn to structure your stories

like a pro

To structure your stories like a pro, it's important to have a clear understanding of the basic storytelling elements and how they fit into the overall structure of the story.

These elements include the beginning, middle, and end of the story, as well as characters, settings, and dialogue.

A common way to structure a story is to use the "story arc" model.

This model consists of five main parts: exposition, conflict, climax, fall, and resolution.

The exposition is where the characters and setting are introduced to the audience, the conflict is where the central problem of the story is presented, the climax is the high point in the story where the conflict is resolved, the fall is where things settle down and the resolution is where the story ends.

Another common structuring technique is the "hero method", which is often used in adventure or fantasy stories.

This method follows the hero's journey as he faces obstacles and learns important lessons along the way.

It's important to remember that a well-structured story must have developed and interesting characters that make the audience care about their journeys.
The choice of setting is also important, as it must be realistic and interesting enough to keep the audience engaged.

Structuring a story should include a strong beginning that grabs the audience's attention and a satisfying ending that brings the story to a satisfying conclusion.

Editing and proofreading are also important parts of structuring, as they allow the writer to refine the story to make it even more engaging and well-structured.

In summary, structuring a story involves understanding the basic elements of the narrative, using structuring techniques such as the story arc and hero method, creating interesting characters and engaging settings, and having a strong beginning and ending. satisfactory.

Create captivating characters that hold the audience's

attention

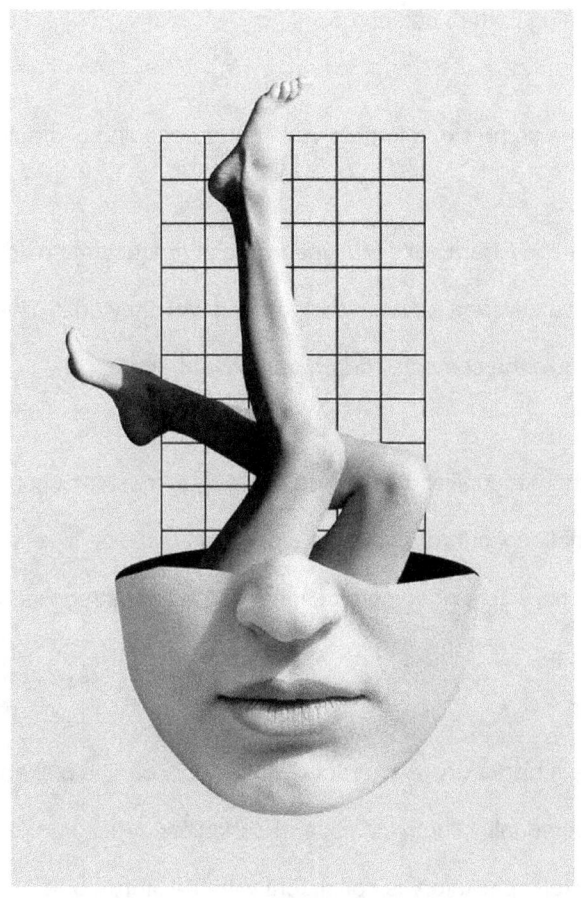

An effective technique for creating endearing characters is to develop characteristics and traits that make them unique and interesting to the audience.

Here are some steps to help you create engaging characters:

Identify the Character's Motivation: Each character should have a clear motivation for what they do and why they do it. This helps give the character depth and a clear purpose.

Give them a conflict: Interesting characters must face conflicts and challenges throughout the story. This could be in relation to other characters or something internal they are struggling to overcome.

Create a backstory: A character's backstory can help shape their personality, motivations, and behaviors. Make sure the character's backstory is consistent with the story's plot.

Give Them Flaws: Perfect, flawless characters can be boring and unrealistic. Give your characters flaws that make them human and make them more interesting to the audience.

Create distinctive dialogue: Your character's dialogue should be distinctive and reflect your personality and motivations. Make sure the dialogue is realistic and consistent with the character's backstory.

Give them a standout look: A character's appearance can be a way to set them apart from other characters. Make sure your appearance is consistent with your personality and background.

When creating endearing characters, it's important to remember that they must be consistent with the plot's story and plot. The characters must also be unique and interesting, with traits that make them memorable and appealing to the audience.

Develop gripping storylines that take audiences on an unforgettable journey

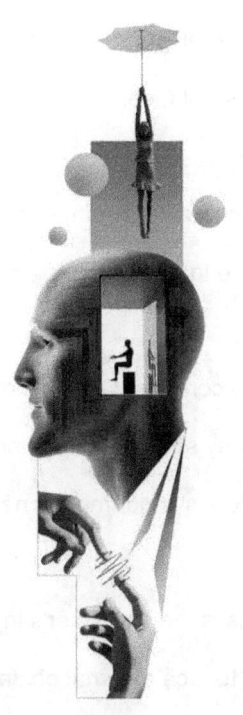

One technique for developing exciting plots is to create meaningful conflicts that take the characters on a transformative journey.

Start by defining the overall purpose of the story and the conflicts the characters will face.

Think about what the characters want to achieve and the obstacles they will have to overcome to achieve their goals.

Then add layers to the conflicts. Conflicts must go deeper than just surface issues. They should be emotional and personal, touching on the characters' fundamental needs and desires.

A good example of this is the character's internal conflict. Instead of just having to face external obstacles, like a villain or a natural catastrophe, the character must also struggle with their own fears, insecurities and personal limitations.

Add unexpected and surprising plot twists.

This keeps the audience engaged and emotionally invested in the story. Twists can also help develop characters by challenging their beliefs and changing their behavior.

Remember that an emotional story should take characters on a transformative journey.

They must come out of history changed and transformed, having learned important lessons and grown emotionally.

To develop exciting plots, start by defining the overall purpose of the story and the conflicts the characters will face.

Finally, make sure the characters go through a transformative journey, learning important lessons and growing emotionally.

Master the art of the twist and keep your audience engaged

until the end

A plot twist is a pivotal moment that can completely change the direction of the plot and surprise the audience.

To master the art of the twist, it's important to follow a few techniques that keep the audience engaged until the end of the story.

The first technique is preparation.

Before introducing the plot twist, it's important to prepare the audience for the moment by including clues and story elements leading up to that moment.

These clues can be small references throughout the story, or even actions that seem insignificant at the time but take on greater importance later on.

The second technique is the internal logic of the story.

The twist should be logical within the story's universe and not seem like a random or convenient solution to a problem.

This ensures that the twist is satisfying for the audience and leaves no questions unanswered.

The third technique is emotion. The twist must be exciting and have a significant impact on the story and characters. The audience must care what happens after the twist and how it affects the characters.

Finally, the plot twist should be a plot point that completely changes the direction of the plot. This ensures that the audience is engaged by the end and eager to see how the story unfolds.

Learn to create settings and environments that make your story come alive

To create vivid settings and environments in your story, it's important to pay attention to detail and create an authentic and immersive sense of place.

Here are some techniques to help bring your settings and environments to life:

Research: Do your research on the environment your story takes place in, be it historical or contemporary. Pay attention to details like the weather, geography, architecture, and local culture.

Use the senses: Include sensory descriptions to help the reader visualize and feel the story's setting.

Describe the smells, sounds, textures and tastes.

Personify the environment: Assign human characteristics to environment elements.

For example, describe the trees as "proud" or the wind as "playful". This helps to give the room a sense of personality.

Use Appropriate Language: Use language that reflects the environment and setting.

For example, if the story takes place in a modern city, use more direct and contemporary language. If the story takes place in a historical setting, use more formal and formal language.

Show, Don't Tell: Rather than simply describing the environment, show it through the characters' actions and reactions.

For example, if a character is walking through a dense forest, point out the difficulty he has moving through the trees and the sound of branches breaking under his feet.

Use the environment to drive the story: Use the environment and setting to help drive the story and characters.

For example, use the weather to build tension, or use the architecture to help reveal information about the characters.

By using these techniques, you can create authentic and engaging settings and environments that will help make your story come alive for the reader.

Develop a captivating and engaging writing style

Developing a captivating and engaging writing style can be a challenging process, but with practice and dedication, you can improve your writing skills.

Here are some techniques to help you develop a writing style that captivates and engages your readers:

Find Your Voice: Find your unique voice as a writer. Write with authenticity and show your personality through your writing style.

Use appropriate language: Use language that reflects your target audience. Use terms appropriate to the topic addressed and use an appropriate tone for the literary genre you are writing.

Maintain consistency: Maintain consistency in your writing style, structure, and narrative voice. This helps keep the reader immersed in the story.

Use literary techniques: Use literary techniques such as metaphor, symbolism, and irony to make writing richer and more engaging.

Review and edit: Review and edit your work frequently. This helps to refine the writing style and improve the quality of the story.

By using these techniques, you can develop a captivating and engaging writing style that will hold your audience's attention and make them want to read more.

Great writers develop their writing styles through a combination of factors such as practice, reading, studying, and experimenting. Here are some common ways writers develop their style:

Practice: Practice is one of the main ways writers develop their style. The more they write, the more they identify their strengths and weaknesses and hone their skills. Over time, they can develop a voice and style of their own.

Reading: Reading is another important way writers can develop their style. By reading a variety of authors and genres, writers can study different writing techniques and develop a deeper understanding of the nuances of the language.

Study: Writers can study specific writing techniques, grammar, and style to hone their skills. They can also study the history of literature and understand how different authors have influenced the development of writing over time.

Experimentation: Writers can experiment with different writing styles, genres, and techniques to find what works best for them. They can also experiment with different forms of storytelling, such as first-person or third-person writing, and different story structures.

Feedback: By getting feedback from other writers and readers, writers can identify areas where they need to improve and find out how their style is perceived by others.

Great writers develop their writing style through a combination of practice, reading, study, experimentation, and feedback.

Style development is an ongoing process that can take years, but can be improved with dedication and effort.

Discover how to use symbols and themes to add depth to your story

Imagine that your story is like a painting, and the symbols and themes are the brushstrokes that add depth and texture to your artwork.

Symbols are like colors that represent ideas and emotions, while themes are like patterns that connect colors and create a bigger picture.

To use this technique, start by selecting the symbols that best represent the main theme of your story.

For example, if your theme is love, choose symbols like hearts, flowers, rings, etc.

Then use these symbols at key moments in the story to emphasize and deepen the theme.

For example, use a broken heart to show a character's grief after a breakup, or a red rose to symbolize the burning passion between two lovers.

Also, use themes that connect the symbols and the overall story.

For example, if the theme of the story is about redemption, use a transformation pattern to show how a character evolves and finds redemption.

Develop subplots: Subplots are side stories that relate to the main plot. They can be used to explore secondary themes that complement the main theme.

By using symbols and themes in your story, you create an extra layer of meaning and depth that can make your work even more engaging and exciting.

Remember to be creative and use your imagination to find the symbols and themes that best represent your story!

The power of combination: How the three parts of the brain work together to wrap us up in a good story.

There are three parts of the brain used for storytelling, which are:

Prefrontal cortex: It is responsible for critical thinking and decision making. It is where the main ideas are formed and where the course of the story is decided.

Limbic system: is responsible for emotions and emotional memory. It is where the emotional bonds between the audience and the story are formed.

Sensory cortex: It is responsible for the senses such as sight, hearing, touch, taste and smell. It's where the sights and sounds of the story are processed and create a sensory experience for the audience.

The prefrontal cortex is the region of the brain responsible for complex cognitive functions such as critical thinking, decision-making, and planning. When we are exposed to stories, this region of the brain is intensely activated, as it is responsible for interpreting the meanings and messages behind the narrative.

By activating the prefrontal cortex, stories are able to evoke emotions, create empathy and convey ideas much more effectively than simple exposure to facts and information. Furthermore, this region of the brain is critical for learning, which explains why stories are so effective at teaching concepts and values.

Research shows that prefrontal cortex activation during story exposure is so intense that people are able to physically feel the characters' emotions and experience the plot as if they were participating in it. This makes the experience of reading a book or watching a movie much more engaging and memorable than simply being exposed to isolated information and facts.

The limbic system is activated by emotional processing and is responsible for regulating emotions, motivation, memory and learning.

When a story is told, several areas of the limbic system are activated, such as the hippocampus, which is responsible for forming memories, the amygdala, which is related to emotional processing and fear regulation, and the nucleus accumbens, which is related to reward and pleasure.

These areas of the limbic system are activated in response to emotional elements in the story, such as conflicts, plot twists, and endearing characters. This can lead to an emotional response from the audience and a greater connection to the story and its characters.

Finally, the sensory cortex is activated by imagination, which is why stories have such an impact on it. When we hear a story, our brain starts creating mental images in response to the words and descriptions we are hearing. For example, if a story describes a scene in a flower garden, the sensory cortex begins to create images of the flowers and scent that we might smell in that environment. This is known as guided imagery.

A study by Emory University found that activation of the sensory cortex during storytelling is similar to the activation that occurs when a person actually experiences a sensory experience.

This means that when we are reading or listening to a story, our brain is not only creating mental images, but it is also activating the same neural circuits that would be activated if we were actually experiencing the sensations described in the story.

But why is this important?

Because activating the sensory cortex makes us more engaged with the story and helps us connect emotionally with the characters and events in the narrative. When we feel the same emotions and sensations that the characters are feeling, our empathy and identification with them increases, which makes us want to keep reading to find out what happens next.

Example:

Let's assume you're reading a thriller. The author describes a scene where the main character is being chased by a murderer. The description is so vivid and detailed that you begin to feel your own breath quicken and your heart beat faster, as if you're being chased too. You're so caught up in the story that you can't stop reading until you find out if the main character manages to escape the killer.

In summary, activation of the sensory cortex by stories is an interesting and important phenomenon for writers and storytellers to understand. When used correctly, guided imagery can take the reader through a full sensory experience,

making the story more engaging and exciting.

Practical tips for revising and editing your story to make it perfect

Reviewing and editing your story is a crucial part of the writing process. Here are some practical tips to help you hone your work to perfection:

Give yourself some time before reviewing: After you finish drafting your story, take some time before you start reviewing.

This will help you see the story with fresher eyes and identify areas that need improvement.

Read aloud: Reading your story aloud helps you spot fluency and grammatical errors that can be overlooked when reading silently.

In addition, it helps to assess the pace of the story and detect parts that can be revised.

Do a general review: Do a first general review to identify and correct errors in grammar, spelling and punctuation.

Make sure the story makes sense and the information is clear.

Check story structure: Make sure the story has a clear, cohesive structure.

Make sure the scenes connect well and the story progression is logical.

Analyze character development:notice if the characters are well developed and if their actions and speeches are consistent with their personality.

Eliminate unnecessary information: unnecessary information or scenes may be dragging the story or not adding anything new.

Ask for opinions: Ask others for their opinions on your story, this can help to identify areas that need more work or that need clarification.

Read again: After reviewing and editing the story, read it again to make sure everything is as it should be.

Remember that proofreading and editing are important processes for improving your story. Don't be afraid to do a lot of revisions and ask for help when needed.

With these practical tips, you can turn your story into a masterpiece.

Create a satisfying ending that leaves the audience

satisfied and thrilled

To create a satisfying ending to a story, it's important to keep in mind the audience's expectations and the message you want to convey. It is critical that all major issues are resolved and that subplots have a coherent outcome.

A common technique is to use "emotional resolution" to give the audience a sense of emotional closure, resolving the characters' internal conflicts and delivering the final message. Another technique is the "final twist", which is a surprising twist that resolves the plot in a unique and unexpected way.

Also, it's important to choose the right tone for the ending of the story. If the plot is dramatic, you can opt for an emotional and reflective ending. If it's an adventure story, an exciting and satisfying ending might be more appropriate.

Finally, it is essential that the end of the story reflects the journey of the characters and the message you want to convey. The audience should leave the story with a sense of satisfaction and a sense of satisfying conclusion.

Conclusion:

Throughout the chapters of "*The Storytelling Architecture*", we learn techniques and strategies to create engaging and exciting stories.

Starting with the importance of understanding the anatomy of the story and the basic structure that underpins it, through creating captivating characters and intriguing plots, and arriving at the art of creating surprising twists and satisfying endings.

We also learned how to develop an engaging writing style and how to use symbols and themes to add depth and meaning to the story. And to make sure our story is the best it can be, we learned practical tips for proofreading and editing our work.

In the end, it's clear that creating an unforgettable story isn't just about telling a story, it's about understanding the journey we want to take our audience on. It's about creating characters that feel real, plots that are challenging and engaging, and endings that meet our emotional expectations. By applying the techniques and strategies presented in this book, we can become better and more effective storytellers and take our readers on an unforgettable journey.